The Waddling Duck

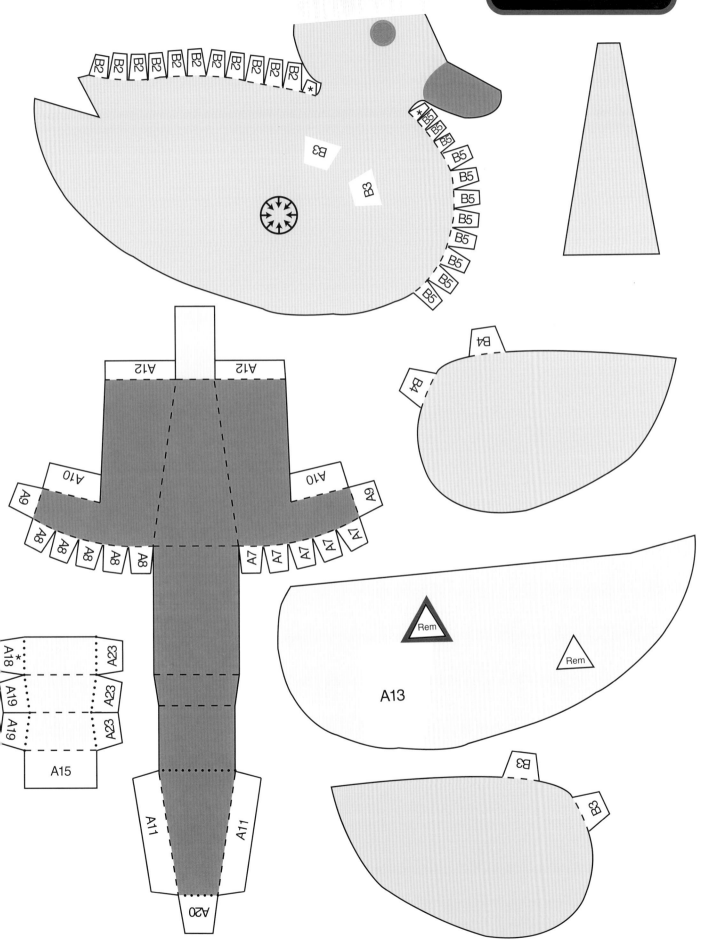

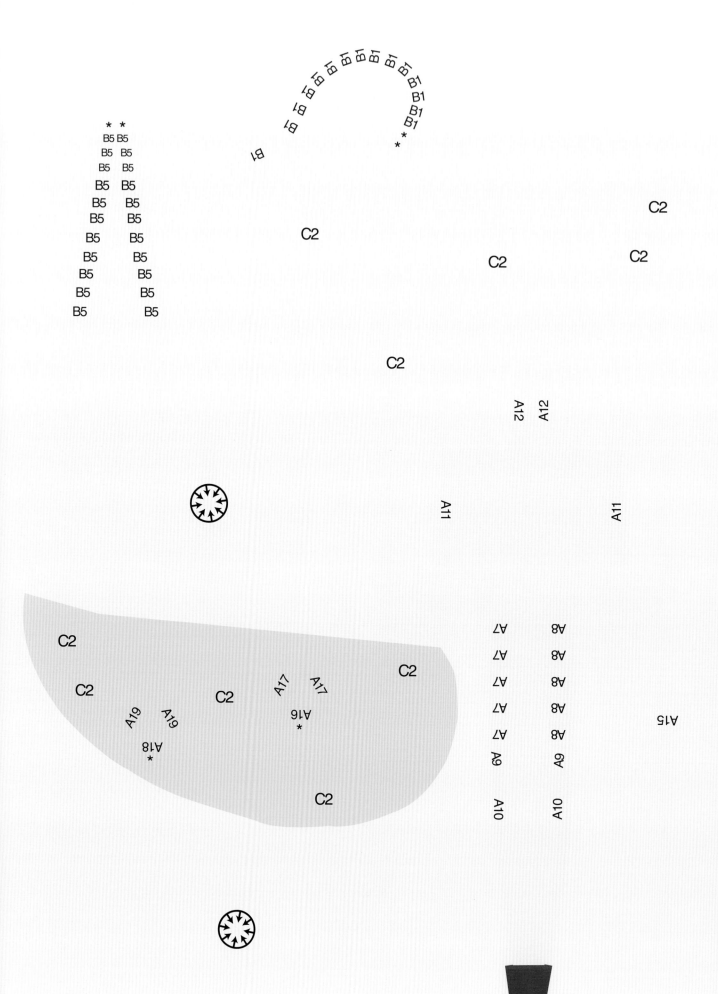

The pair of Orange and Yellow Ducklings are on pages 29 & 31.

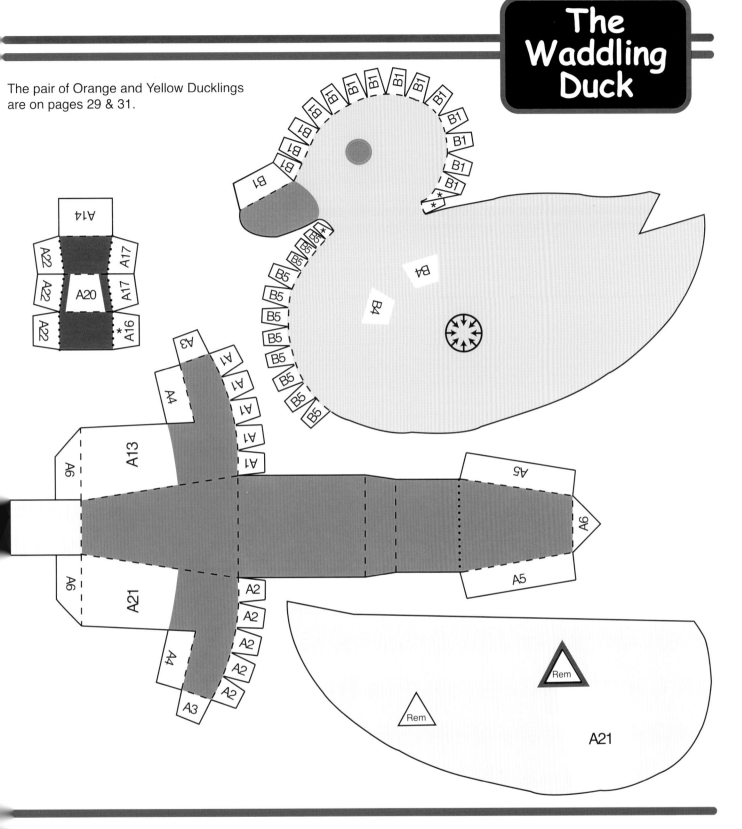

This piece is the deck for the Ark. See also pages 5, 7 & 9.

The Noah's Ark

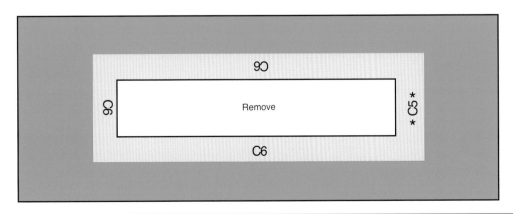

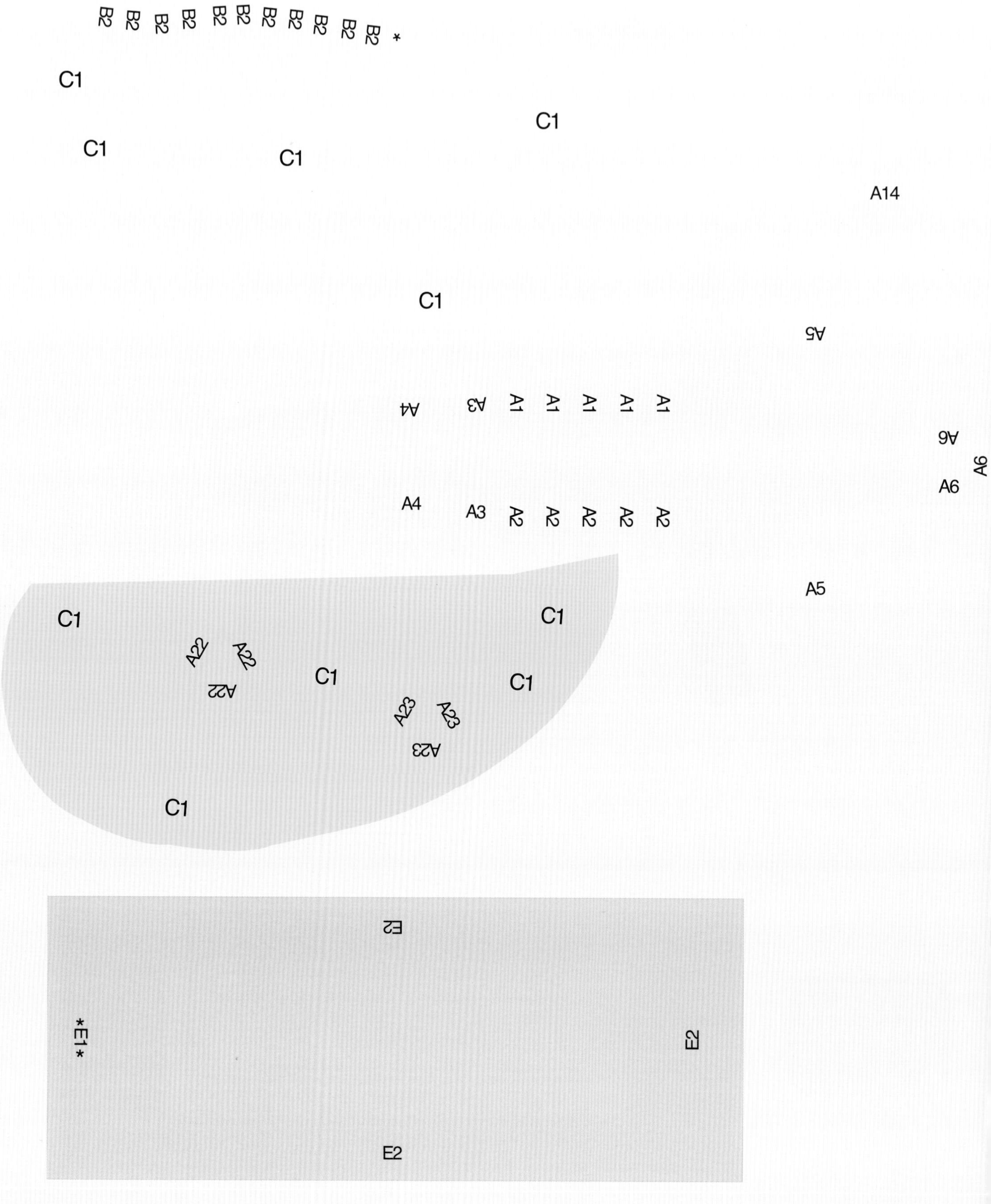

B2 B2 B2 B2 B2 B2 B2 B2 B2 B2 *

C1

C1

C1

C1

C1

A14

C1

A5

A4 A3 A1 A1 A1 A1 A1

A6
A6
A6 A6

A4 A3 A2 A2 A2 A2 A2

A5

C1 C1

A22 A22

C1 C1

A22

A23 A23

A23

C1

E2

E1

E2

E2

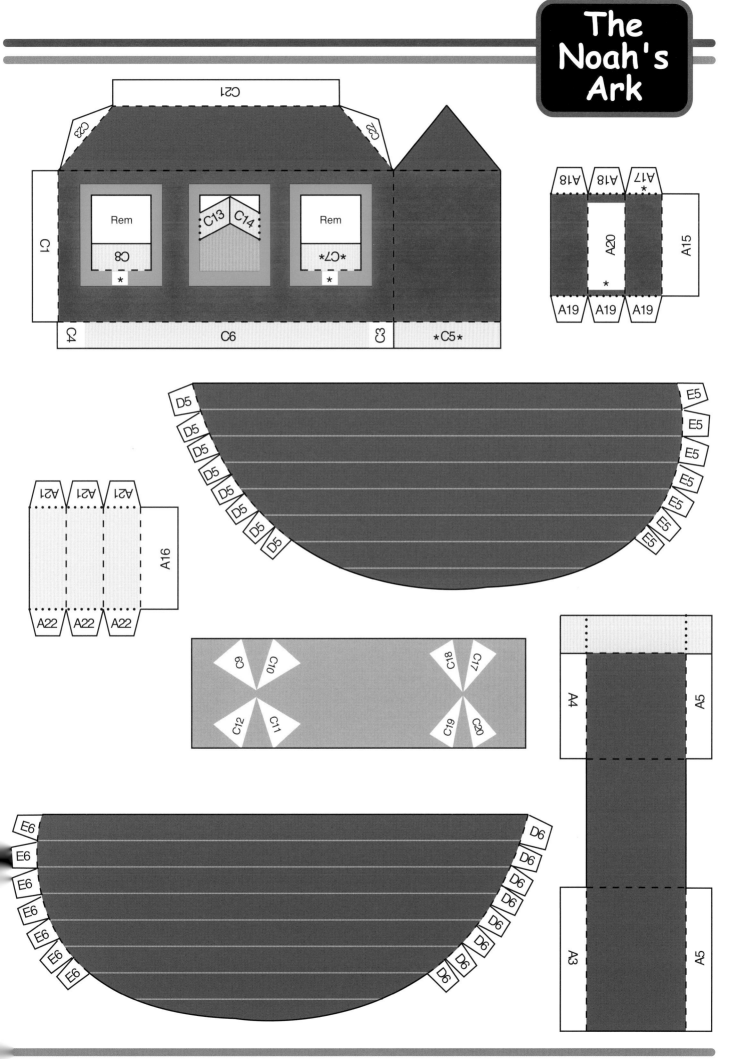

C3 C2

C2

A15

C3 C3

D3

A16

A7

A6

* C7 *

C8

* C7 *

C8

A2 A1
A2 A1
A2 A1
A2 A1
A2 A1

D4

See page 3 for the deck which is needed to complete the Ark.

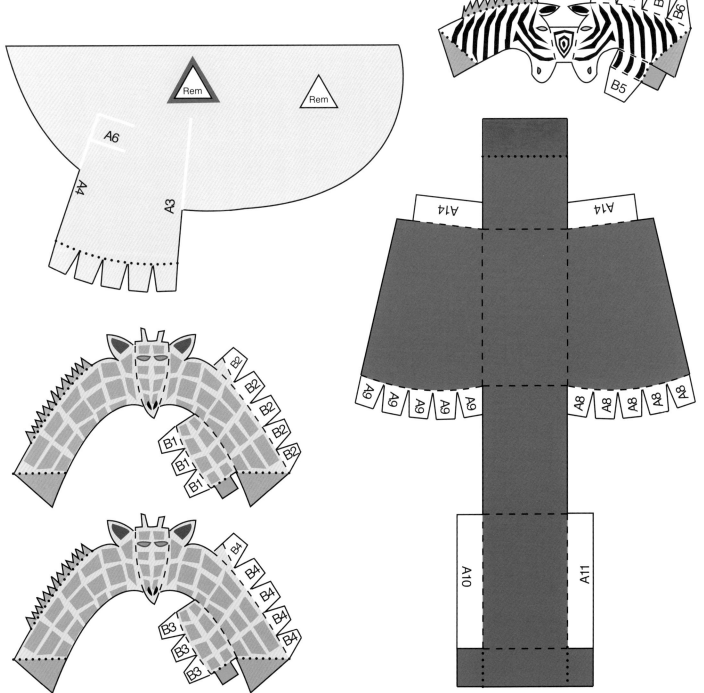
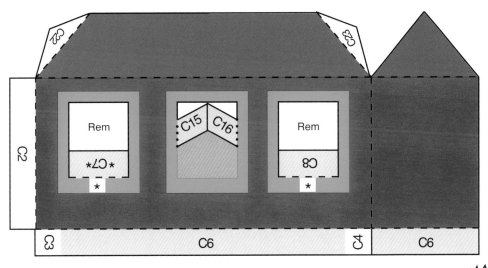

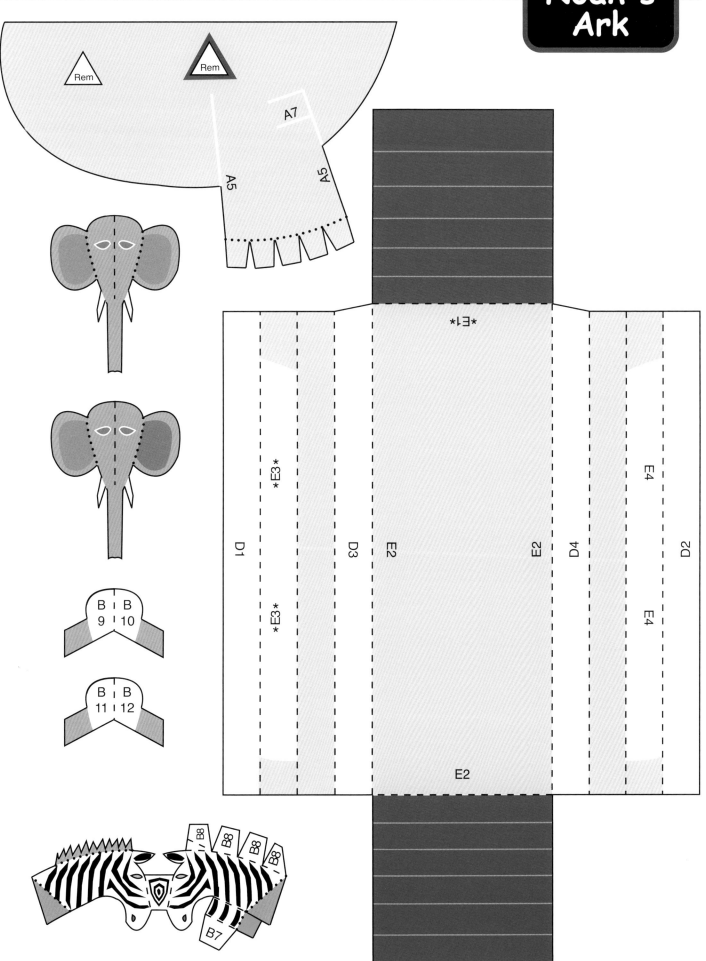

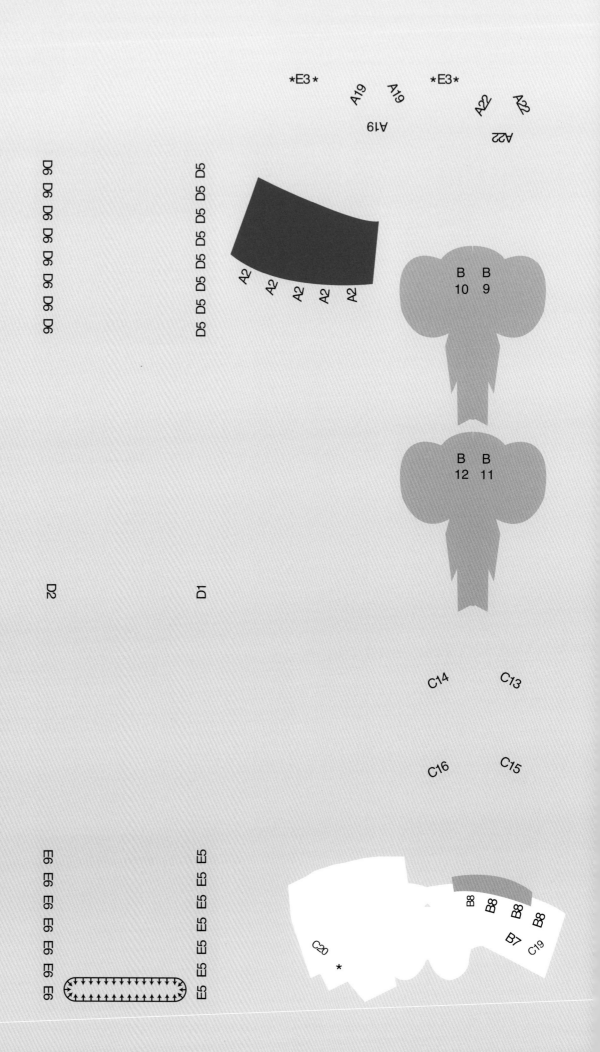

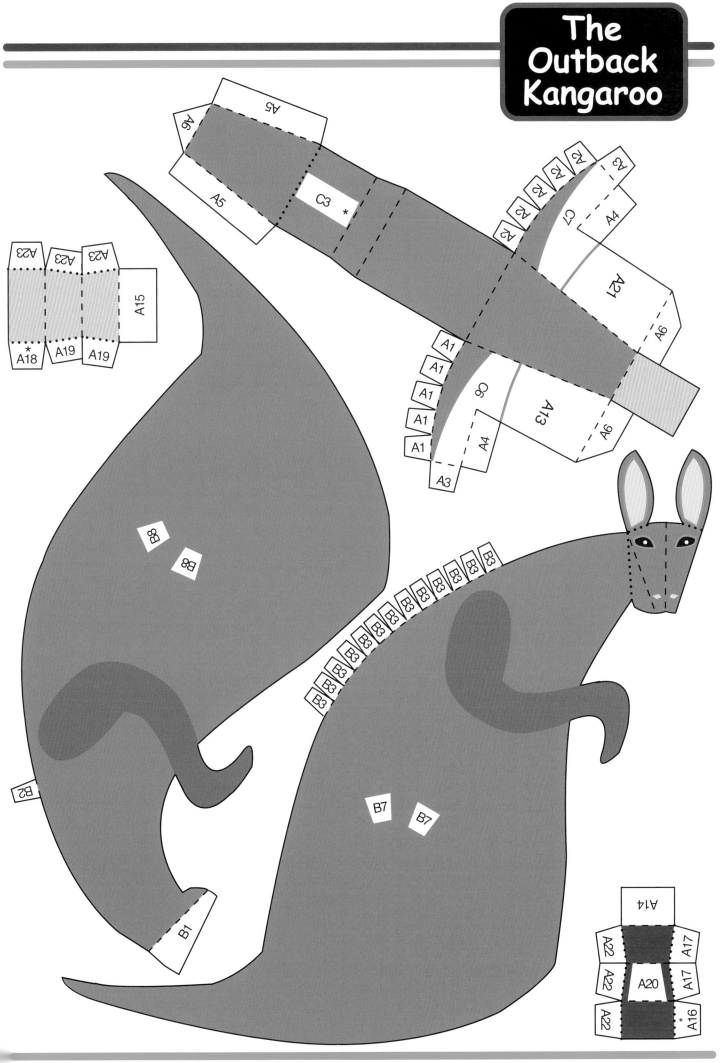

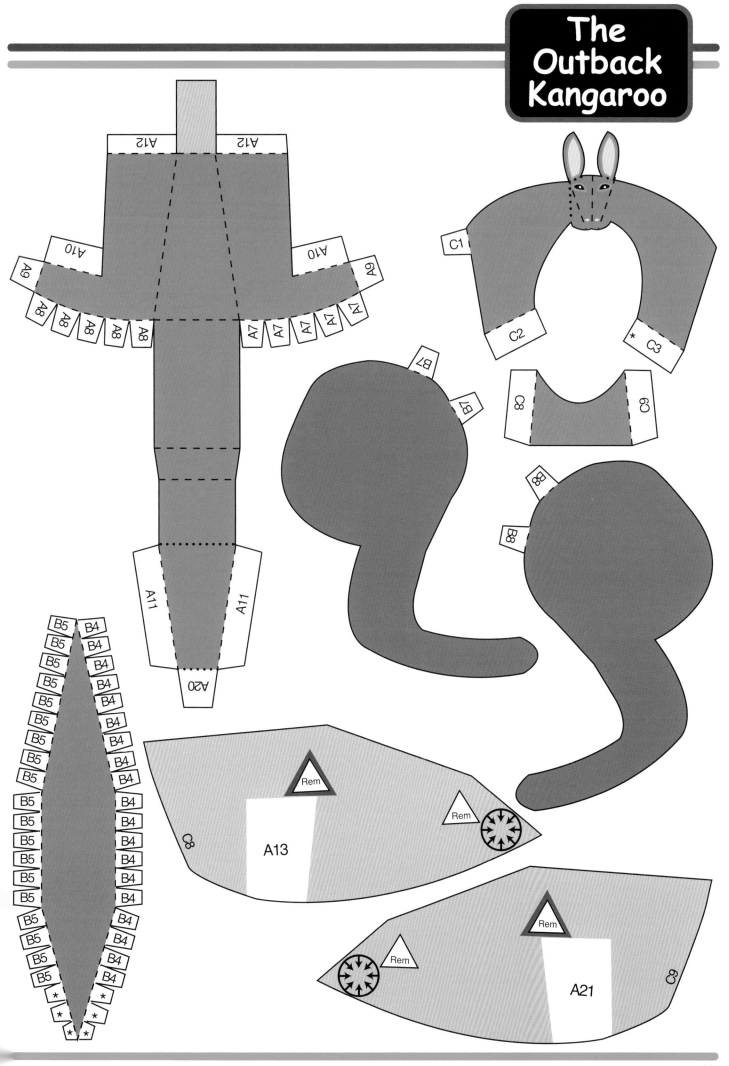

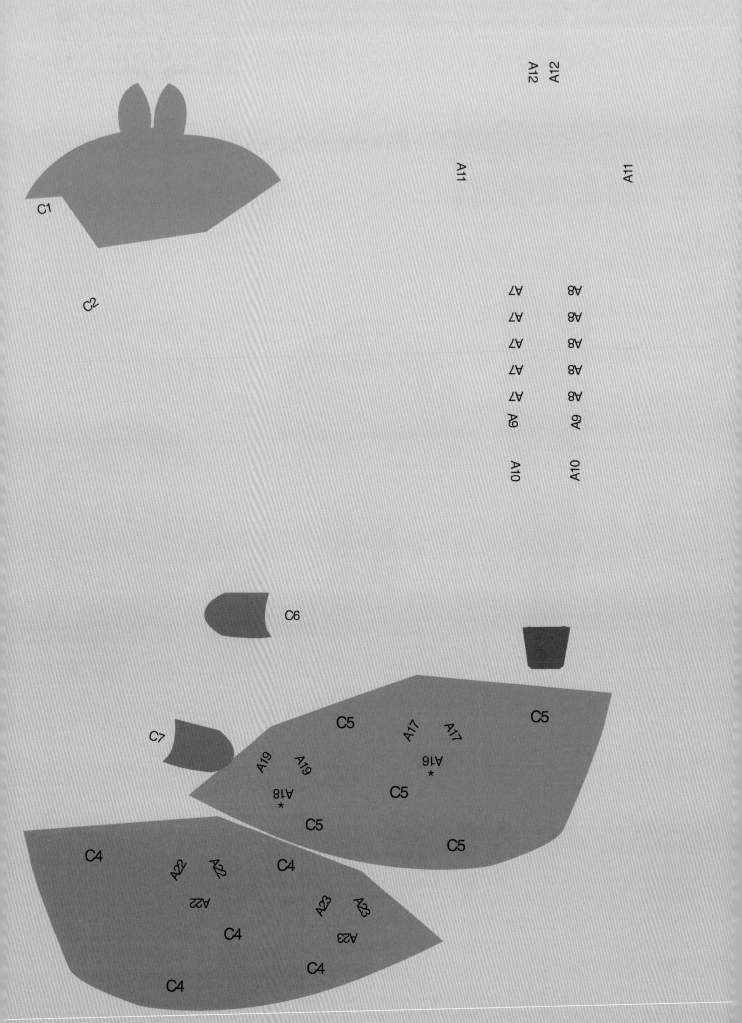

See inside the front cover for instructions about scoring, cutting out and folding and also the type of glue to use. Each of the walking automata has a similar mechanism at its heart and it is best to start by making that unit. Because there are slight differences, they are divided into two groups, called 'Type X' and 'Type Y'.

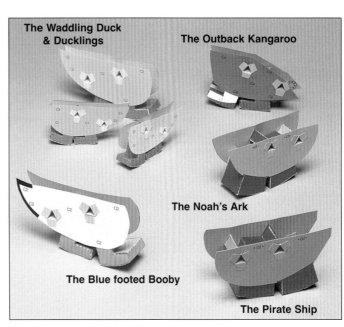

The Waddling Duck & Ducklings	The Outback Kangaroo
	The Noah's Ark
The Blue footed Booby	The Pirate Ship

The Seven Mechanisms

The Walking Mechanisms   Type X

The Waddling Ducks

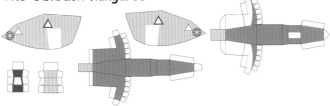

These are the pieces for the waddling duck.
For the two ducklings, the shapes and numbering are the same but the size and colours are different.

The Outback Kangaroo

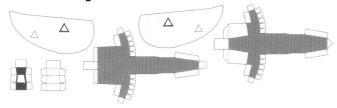

The Blue footed Booby

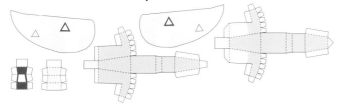

Start by identifying the six pieces needed for each of the mechanisms shown above.
Then glue tabs A1 to A23 working in numerical order.

A1 - A6: Make the fixed foot.
A7 - A12: Make the moving foot.
A13: Glue the first side of the fixed foot into position.
A14, A15: Make the pivot bar (red) and the back stop.
A16, A17: Push the pivot bar tabs through the pivot bar hole (red) and then glue into position carefully matching A16.
A18, A19: Push the backstop tabs through the backstop hole and then glue into position carefully matching A18.
A20: Glue the moving foot into position.
* Push the tabs marked A22 and A23 through their corresponding holes.*
A21: Glue the second side of the fixed foot into position.
A22, A23: Glue the tabs of the pivot bar and the back stop.

Finally check that the moving foot swings freely.

The Walking Mechanisms   Type Y

The Noah's Ark

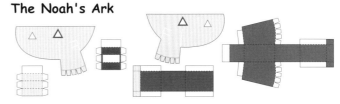

The Pirate Ship

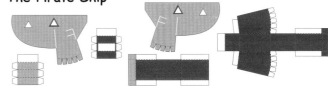

Start by identifying the six pieces needed for each of the mechanisms as shown above.
Then glue tabs A1 to A22 working in numerical order.

A1 - A7: Assemble the fixed foot and the mechanism sides.
A8 - A14: Make the moving foot.
A15, A16: Make the pivot bar (red) and the back stop.
A17, A18, A19: Push the tabs through the pivot bar holes (red) and glue in position carefully matching A17.
*A20: Glue the moving foot into position, so that the * s match.*
A21, A22: Push the tabs through the backstop holes and then glue them into position.

Finally check that the moving foot swings freely.

To complete the models see page 16 and 17.

Completing the models ...

The Waddling Duck — Type X

The Body

First identify these five pieces.
Then make this unit by glueing tabs B1 to B5 in order.

B1 - B2: Glue the two halves together starting with the beak and the head and finishing along the spine.
B3, B4: Glue the wings to the sides.
B5: Gently curve the breast and then glue it into position.

Final Assembly

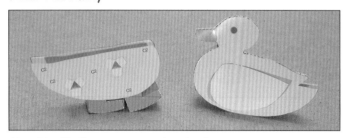

Now identify these two completed units.

C1, C2: Slide the body over the walking unit and glue it to both sides.

The Blue footed Booby — Type X

The Body

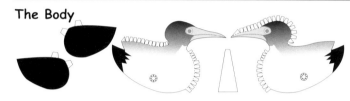

First identify these five pieces.
Then make this unit by glueing tabs B1 to B5 in order.

B1 - B2: Glue the two halves together starting with the beak and the head and finishing along the spine.
B3, B4: Glue the wings to the sides.
B5: Gently curve the breast and then glue it into position.

Final Assembly

Now identify these two completed units.

C1, C2: Slide the body over the walking unit and glue it to both sides.

The Outback Kangaroo — Type X

The Body

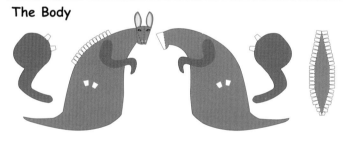

First identify these five pieces.
Then make this unit by glueing tabs B1 to B8 in order.

B1: Join the two sides together by glueing at the head.
B2, B3: Turn the head a little sideways and then glue along the shoulders.
B4 - B6: Gently curve the back and then glue into place, right to the end of the tail.
B7, B8: Glue both legs to the body.

Final Assembly

 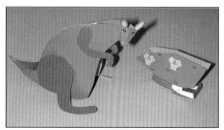

Now identify these two pieces and the two completed units.

C1, C2: Make the joey.
C3: Glue the joey to the walking unit.
C4, C5: Slide the walking unit inside the body and glue it to both sides.
C6, C7: Glue the legs to both sides of the fixed foot.
C8, C9: Glue the pouch into position.

The Ducklings — Type X

The Body   The Body

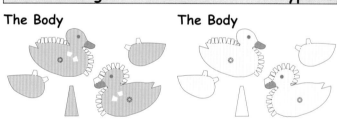

To make each duckling follow the instructions for the Waddling Duck at the top of the page.

To prepare the models for walking see page 18.

Completing the models ...

The Noah's Ark Type Y

The Animals

First identify these eight pieces.
Then make the animals by glueing tabs B1 to B12 in order.

B1 - B4: Make the two giraffe heads.
B5 - B8: Make the two zebra heads.
B9 - B12: Glue the two elephant heads to their inner layers.

The Animals' Quarters

First identify these four pieces.
Then make this unit by glueing tabs C1 to C23 in order.

C1 - C6: Join the two sides and add them to the base, making sure that the C5's match.
C7, C8: Add the internal floor making sure that the C7's match. Now add the six completed animals.
C9 - C20: Glue them into position with their heads looking outwards through the windows.
C21 - C23: Complete the roof.

The Hull of the Ark

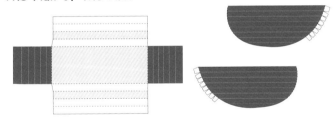

First identify these three pieces.
Then make this unit by glueing tabs D1 to D6 in order.

D1, D2: Make the two deck supports.
D3, D4: Glue the sides to the deck.
D5, D6: Glue the prow into position.

Final Assembly

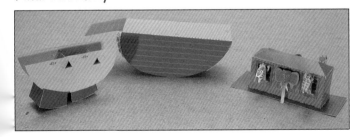

Now identify these three completed units.

E1, E2: Glue the animals' quarters and the hull of the ark together making sure that the E1's match.
E3, E4: Add the walking mechanism, making sure that the E3's match.
E5, E6: Close the stern.

The Pirate Ship Type Y

The Hull of the Ship

First identify these eight pieces.
Then make this unit by glueing tabs B1 to B26 in order.

B1 - B4: Roll the cannon barrels around a pen or pencil and then glue them together.
B5 - B12: Push the cannons through ship's sides, taking care that the B5's, B7's, B9's, B11's match. The asterisks help.
B13: Join the two sides to make the prow of the ship.
B14, B15: Make the deck supports.
B16 - B20: Add the sides of ship to the deck supports.
B21 - B26: Construct the cabin area.

The Masts and Deck

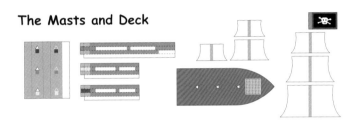

First identify these twelve pieces.
Then make this unit by glueing tabs C1 to C18 in order.

C1 - C3: Make the three masts. Push the masts through the holes in the masts support, carefully matching C4 - C9.
C4 - C9: Glue the masts in position within the masts support.
C10: Close and complete the masts support. Push the deck over the three masts.
C11: Glue the masts support to the underside of the deck.
C12 - C18: Glue the sails and the flag to the masts.

Final Assembly

Now identify these three completed units.

D1: Glue the deck and sails to the hull of the ship.
D2, D3: Add the walking unit, making sure that the D2's match
D4, D5: Close the stern.

To prepare the models for walking see page 18.

Preparing the models for walking ...

1. Setting up the slope

*For the models to walk, they need to be on a suitable slope.
A convenient length is from 30cm to 40cm.*

*The slope should be at about 12° to the horizontal. This
means a rise of 1cm for every 5cm on the slope.*

*The surface should not be too slippery or too rough.
Experiment! A cork notice-board or a cork tray makes a very
quick and easy slope to set up. If the cork is right that is all
you need to do. If not, try placing a sheet of photocopy paper
on it, white or coloured. Another thing to try is to cover a short
plank or a shelf with a fine teacloth.*

2. Adjusting the balance

*To walk properly, the centre of gravity of each of the models
needs to be in just the right place. Make the fine adjustments
with Blu-Tak or a similar plasticine-like material.*

*These symbols show where the Blu-Tak should be added and
their size indicates roughly how much is needed. There should
be equal amounts on both sides for the models to balance.*

*The Kangaroo also has a small piece at the back of the neck.
For the Ark and the Pirate's Ship, the Blu-Tak is all at the stern,
on both sides and across the back.*

*All the models walk beautifully with a charming 'clicking sound'
when they are properly weighted. If any of yours do not, then
it is a case of making slight adjustments until they do. Add or
take away small amounts of Blu-Tak from the suggested sites.*

*There is a certain knack in placing the models on the slope to
start them off, but this is less important than correct weighting.
In any case you will quickly acquire the knack!*

3. Special attention needed

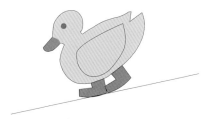

*Always check that the moving foot really does move freely. Be
careful when adding the Blu-Tak not to squash the sides on to
the foot. Use scissors or a small ruler to press against.*

4. How do they walk?

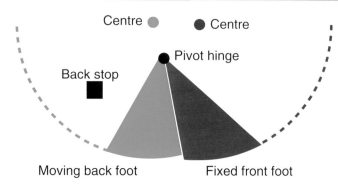

*The base of each foot is in the shape of an arc of a circle and
the centres of these arcs are marked on the diagram.
Only the back foot (green) is able to move relative to the rest
of the model. It has a paper hinge which acts as a pivot and
allows it to move back and forth.*

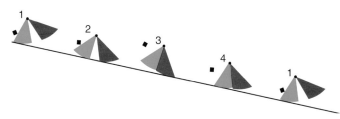

1. To start off, the moving foot is back against the backstop
   and the fixed foot is in the air.
2. The whole model rocks forward and the weight is
   transferred to the front foot.
3. The moving foot swings forward until it hits the fixed foot
   making a clicking sound.
4. The model then rocks backwards causing the weight to be
   transferred back on to the moving foot just before it hits the
   backstop.

*So it continues 1, 2, 3, 4, 1, 2, 3, 4, 1 .....
until the model reaches the bottom of the slope.*

To design models of your own see inside back cover.

The Blue footed Booby

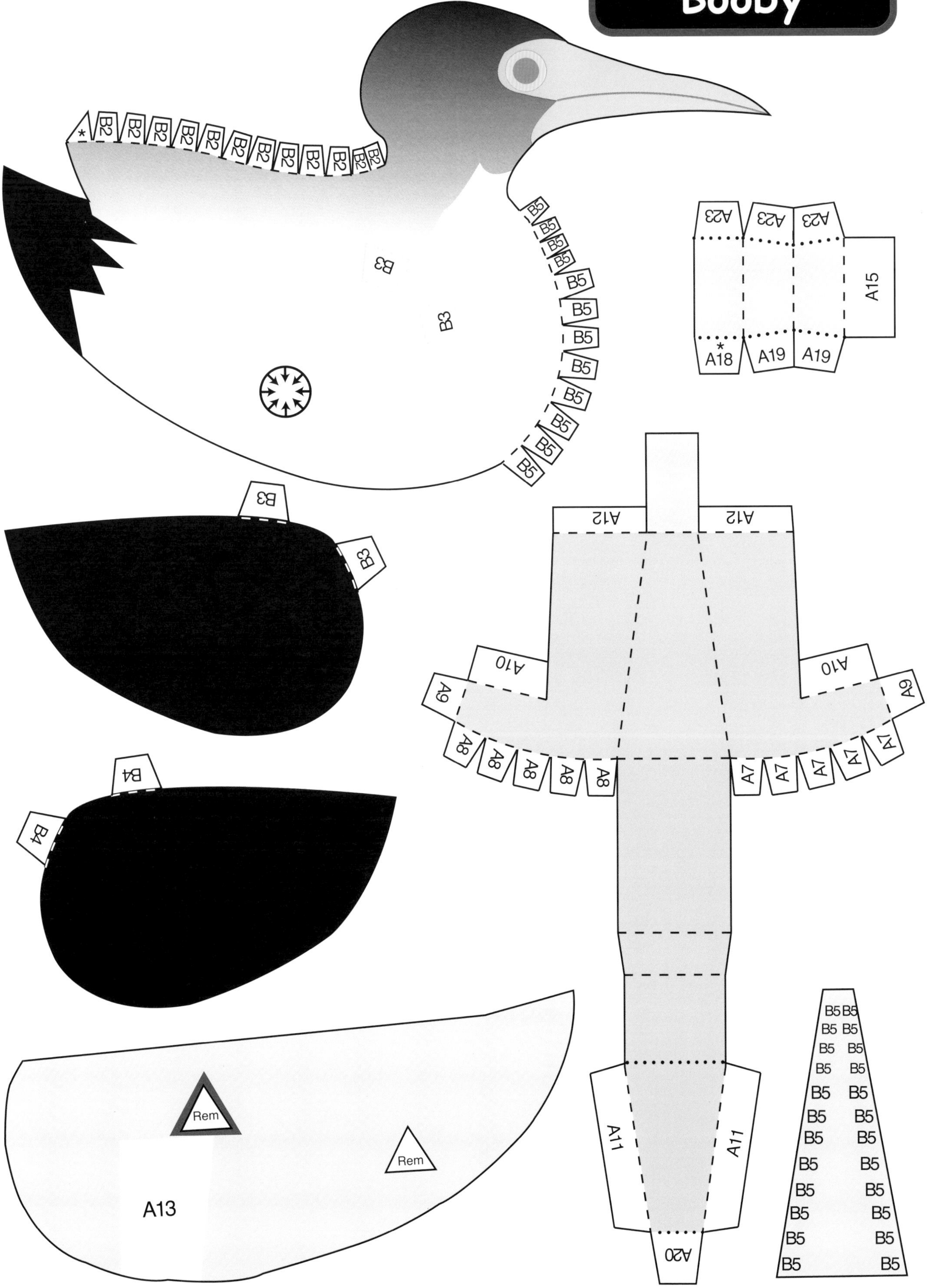

B2 B2 B2 B2 B2 B2 B2 B2 B2 B2 B2 *

B5 B5 B5 B5 B5 B5 B5 B5 B5 B5 B5 B5 B5 B5

B3

B3

A23 A23 A23

A15

A18 * A19 A19

B3

B3

B4

B4

A12 A12

A10 A10

A9 A9

A8 A8 A8 A8 A8 A7 A7 A7 A7 A7

A11 A11

A20

Rem

Rem

A13

B5 B5
B5 B5
B5 B5
B5 B5
B5 B5
B5 B5
B5 B5
B5 B5
B5 B5
B5 B5
B5 B5
B5 B5

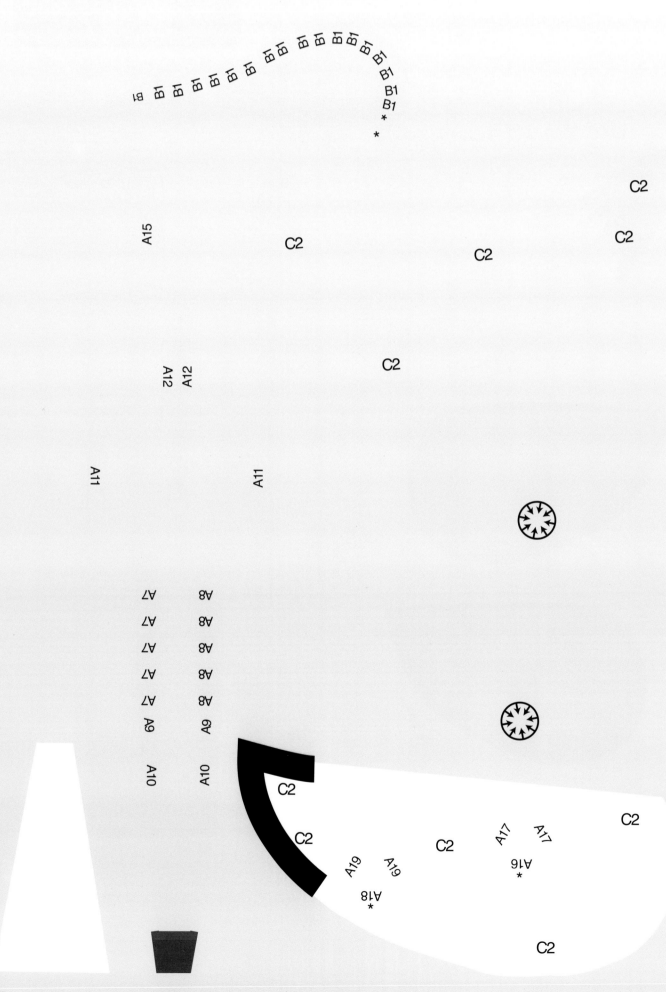

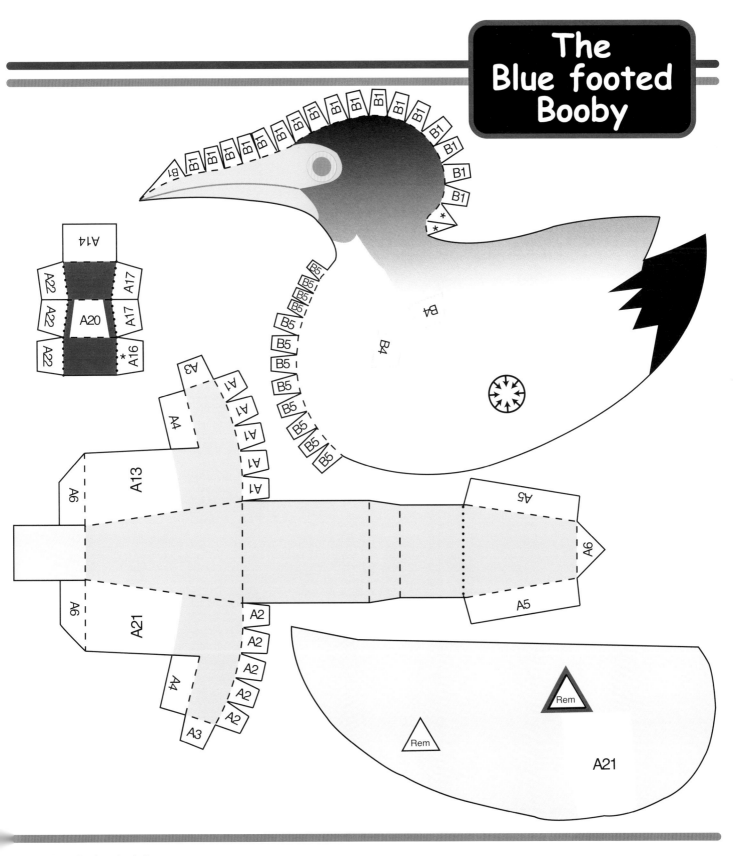

The Blue footed Booby

This piece is the deck for the Pirate Ship. See also pages 23, 25 & 27.

The Pirate Ship

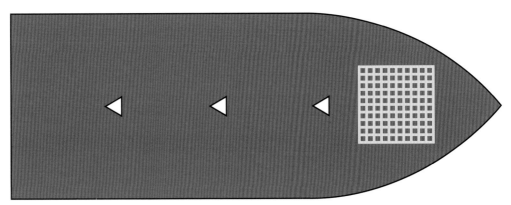

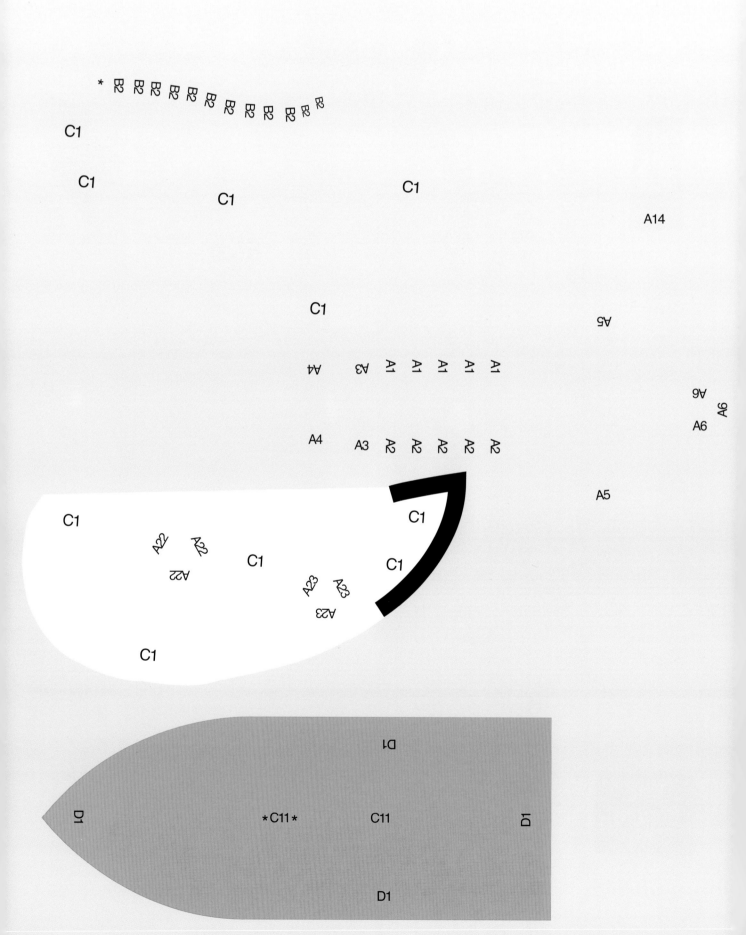

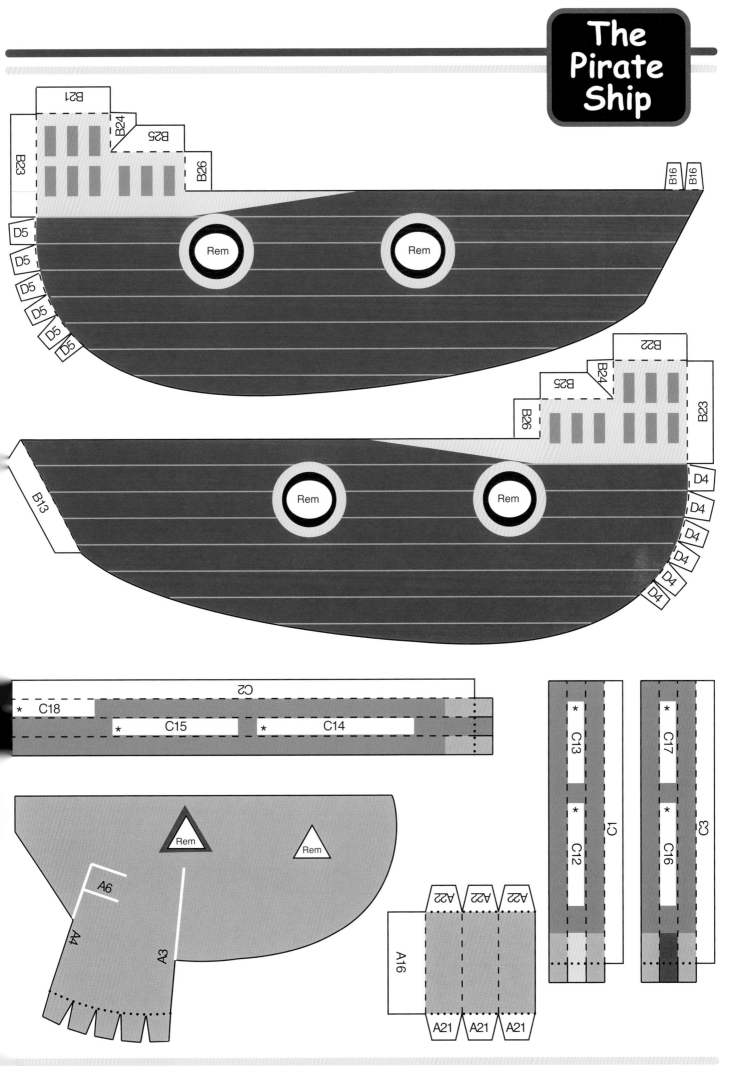

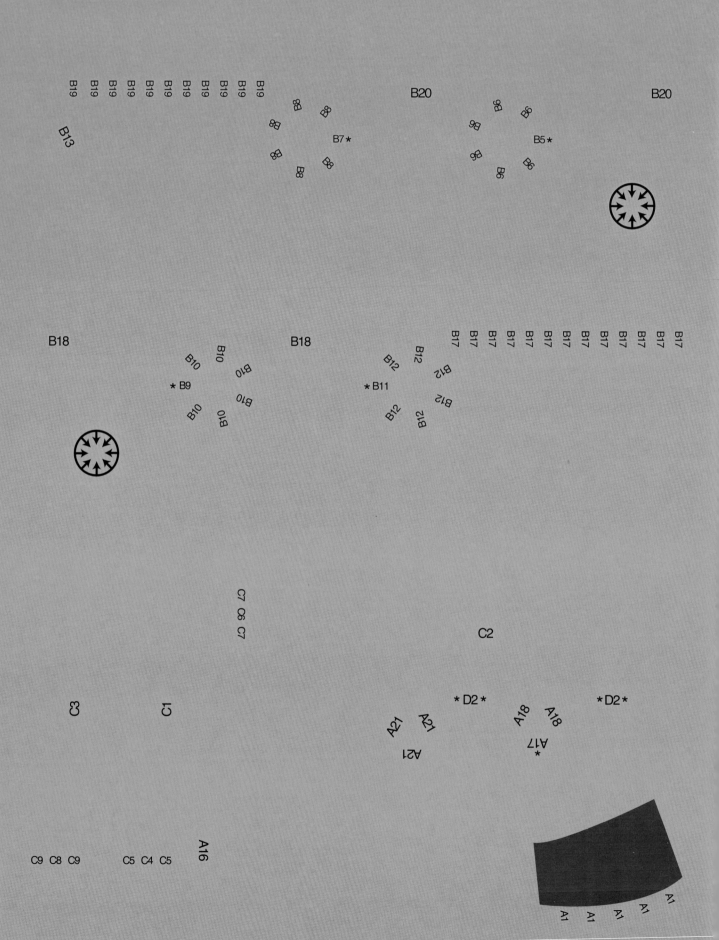

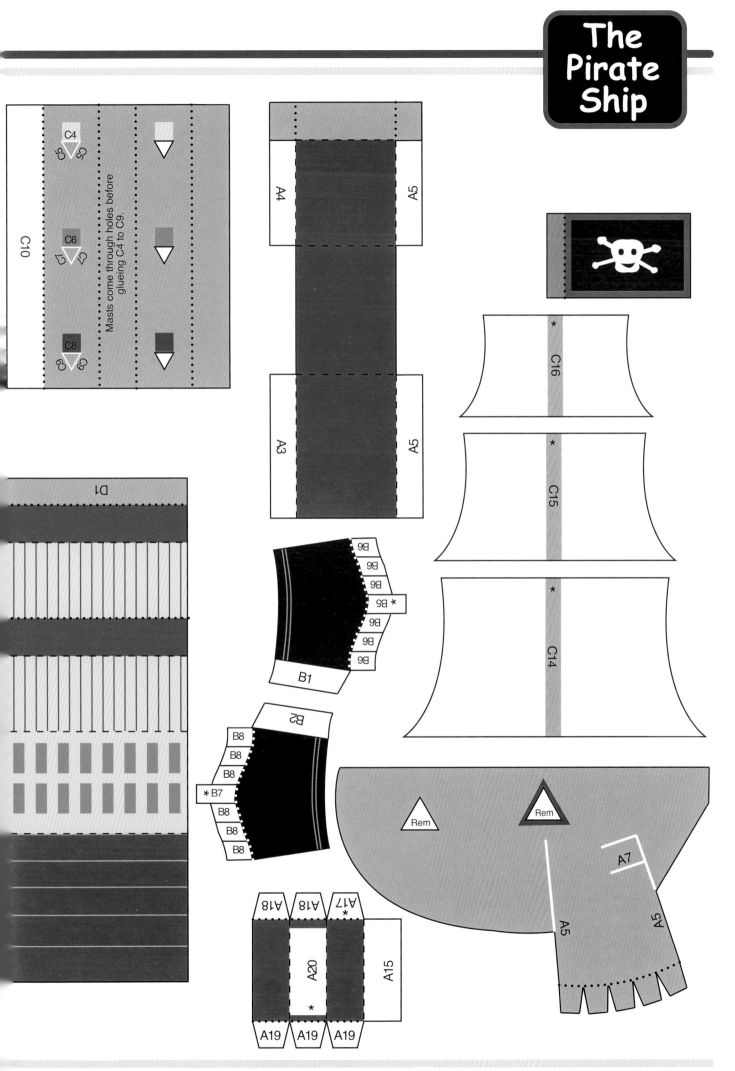

Masts come through holes before glueing C4 to C9.

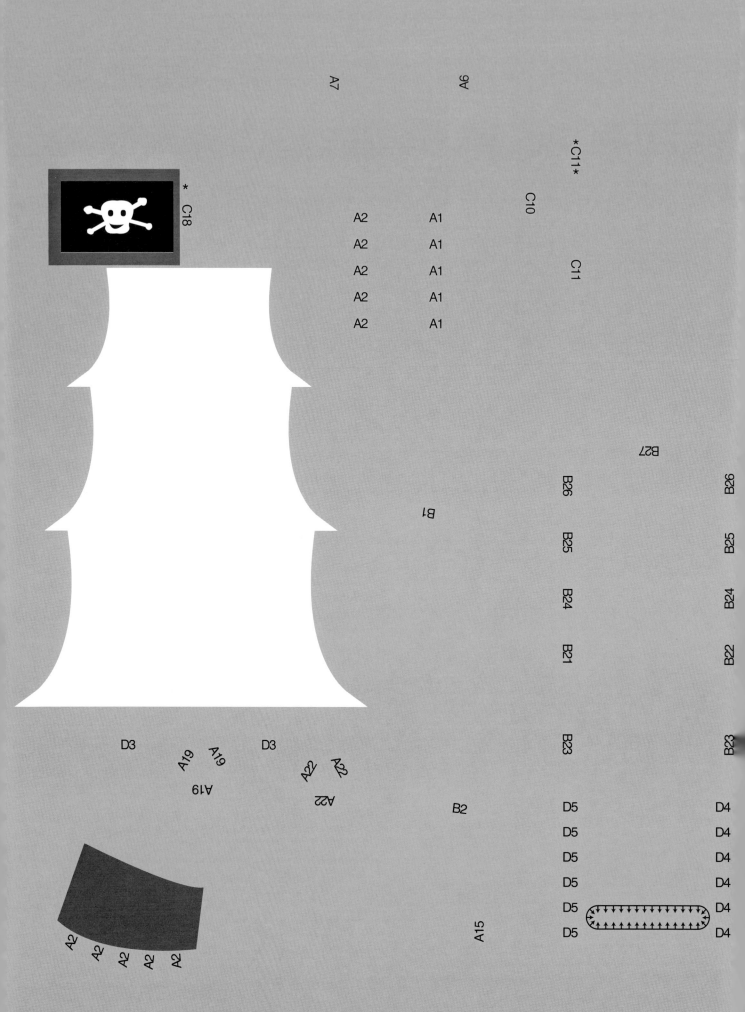

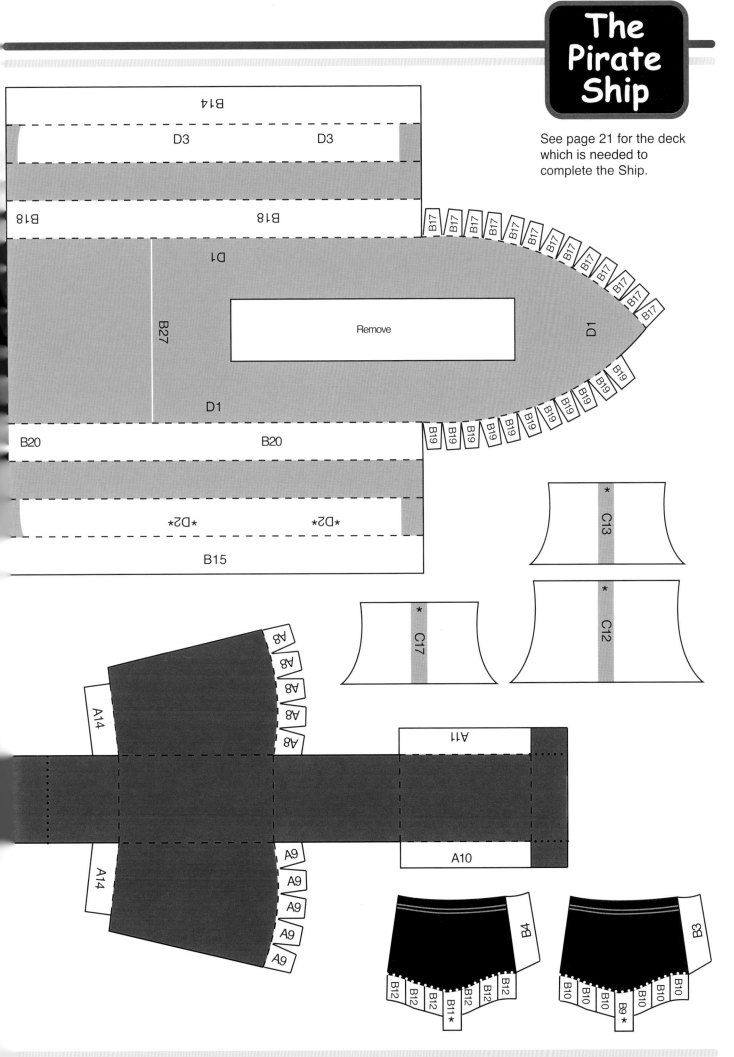

See page 21 for the deck which is needed to complete the Ship.

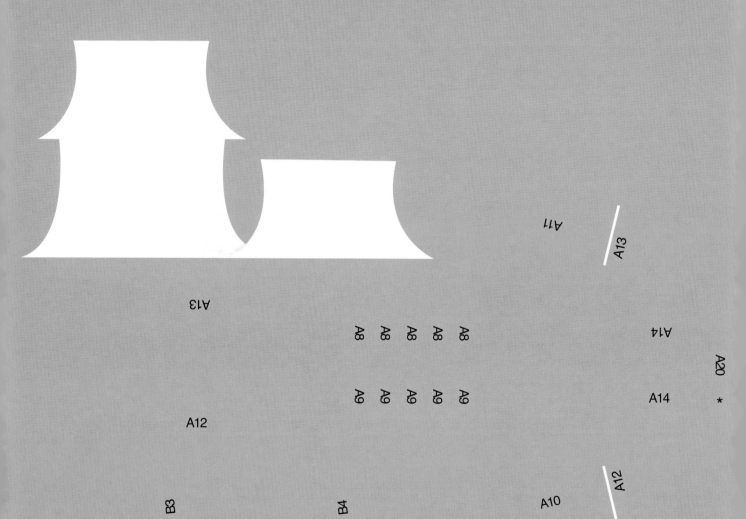

B4

A10

A1

A10

B14

B16
B16

B15

A11

A13

A13

A14

A8 A8 A8 A8 A8

A20

A9 A9 A9 A9 A9

A14

A12

*

A12

B3

B4

A10

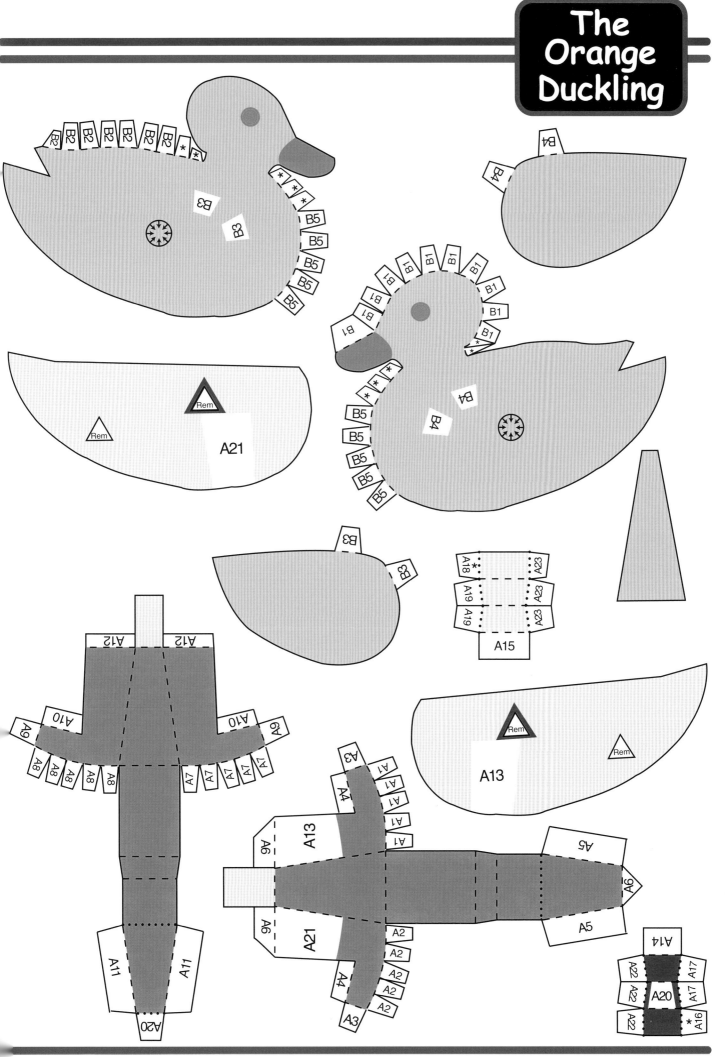

The Orange Duckling

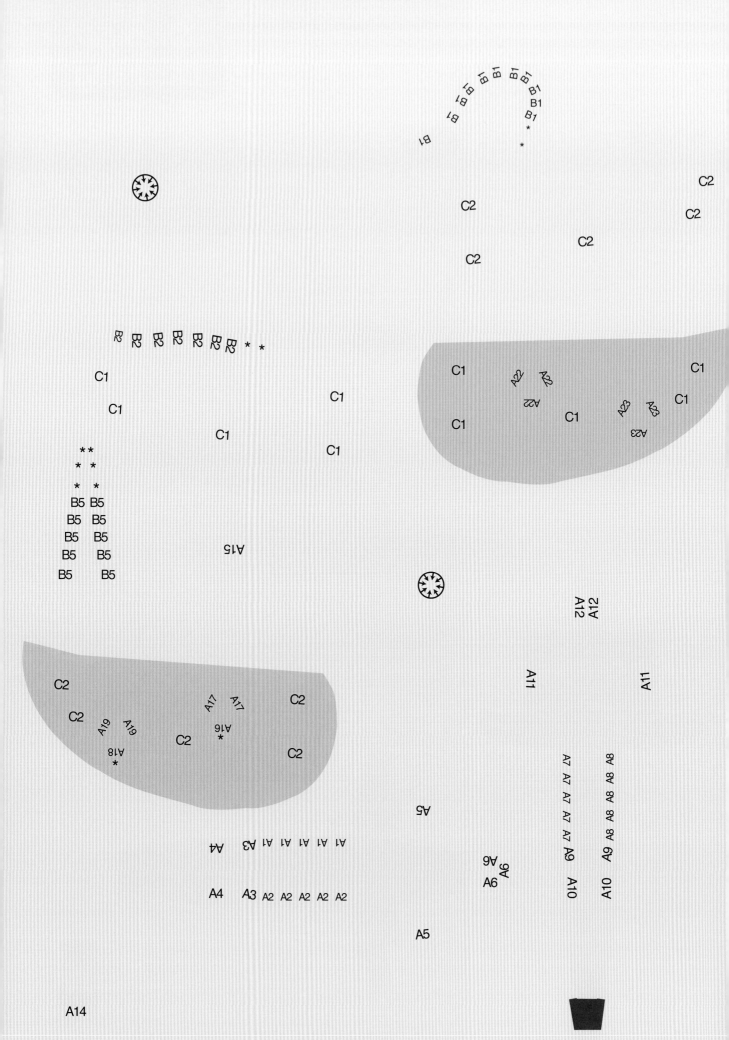

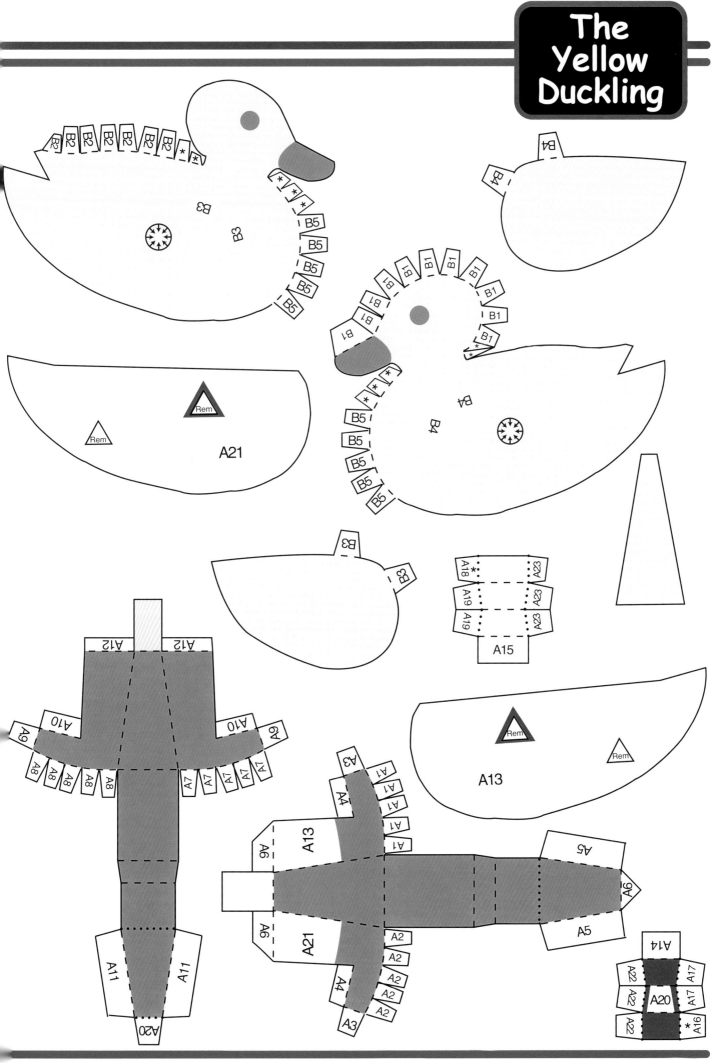

B1 B1 B1 B1 B1 B1 B1 B1 B1 B1
*
*

C2

C2

C2

C2

C2

B2 B2 B2 B2 B2 B2 B2 B2 * *

C1

C1

C1

C1

C1

C1

C1

C1

C1

A22 A22 A22

A23 A23 A23

* *
* *
* *
B5 B5
B5 B5
B5 B5
B5 B5
B5 B5

A15

A12
A12

A11

A11

C2

C2

C2

A19 A19

A17 A17

A16
*

A18
*

C2

C2

A7 A7 A7 A7 A7 A8 A8 A8 A8 A8

A5

A9 A8 A8 A9

A6 A6
A6 A6

A10 A10

A5

A1 A1 A1 A1 A3

A4

A4 A3 A2 A2 A2 A2 A2

A5

A14